VASCO DA GAMA

The Portuguese Quest for a Sea Route from Europe to India

Allison Stark Draper

the rosen publishing group's
rosen
central

For my father

Published in 2003 by The Rosen Publishing Group, Inc.
29 East 21st Street, New York, NY 10010

First Edition

Library of Congress Cataloging-in-Publication Data

Draper, Allison Stark.
Vasco da Gama : the Portuguese quest for a sea route from Europe to India / Allison Stark Draper.
    p. cm. — (The library of explorers and exploration)
Includes bibliographical references (p.   ).
Summary: Describes the fifteenth century voyages taken by Portuguese explorer Vasco da Gama who furthered his nation's power by expanding trade routes to India.
ISBN 0-8239-3632-5 (lib. bdg.)
1. Gama, Vasco da, 1469–1524—Journeys—Juvenile literature.
2. Explorers—Portugal—Biography—Juvenile literature.
3. Discoveries in geography—Portuguese—Juvenile literature.
[1. Gama, Vasco da, 1469–1524. 2. Explorers.]
I. Title. II. Series.
G286.G2 D725 2002
910'.92—dc21

J 910.92
G184
[B]

2001007018

Manufactured in the United States of America

CONTENTS

Admiral Dom Vasco da Gama was the count of Vidigueira and sixth governor and second viceroy of India. Unlike many explorers in his time, da Gama actually profited from his voyages during his lifetime. He was granted titles of nobility, a large pension, and even an estate of significant wealth.

INTRODUCTION

HEROES AND VILLAINS

Fifteenth-century European sailors braved violent storms, navigated razor-sharp reefs, and suffered the painful disease scurvy. They fought the wild beasts and the hostile soldiers of foreign shores. The terrors that men faced at sea are almost unimaginable. Sea captains strong enough or lucky enough to sail home with foreign gold and the promise of new sea routes became legendary. Vasco da Gama, the navigator who charted the sea route from Portugal to India, is one of the most celebrated figures in the history of European exploration. Born in Portugal roughly thirty years into the country's exploration contributions, he was perfectly placed to become a hero.

The difference between a hero and a villain, however, is not always clear. On one hand, in his determination to reach the treasures of the East, da Gama performed acts so monstrous that he sometimes alarmed his own crews, callous as they were. On the other hand, da Gama's voyage opened up a world that had been completely unavailable to Renaissance Portugal. Through his success, his country achieved wealth and became a world power. Da Gama's atrocities were unknown to most people. In those years, the Portuguese citizens idolized da Gama for bringing Portugal to the attention of the world. The commercial sea trade that he charted helped the country build an empire in the East, reaching Indonesia by 1512 and China by 1514.

But da Gama was not an isolated hero. He was the product of nearly a century of Portuguese ambition. In the decades before his birth, Portugal had made a plan. Its kings believed that profit and power lay in the East. At that time, Indian luxuries such as silk and cinnamon filtered into Europe slowly and expensively. Because the Portuguese had no hope of traveling to India across the lands that lay through the Middle East, they decided to search for a sea route. Their only obstacle was the African continent. The arid stretches of the Sahara desert, the chaotic sea winds off the coast, and superstition convinced many that, near the equator, the sea boiled. Some people even believed that hideous sea monsters inhabited the southern oceans!

One of Portugal's princes, Henry the Navigator, scoffed at these stories. He had read ancient accounts of sea voyages around Africa. With these historical accounts in mind, he spearheaded the development of Portuguese oceanic navigation. This enabled ships to navigate in the open sea instead of hugging the coasts as they traveled.

All that remained was to send a fleet around the southern tip of Africa (later named the Cape of Good Hope) and up into the Indian Ocean. Da Gama captained the ship that seventy-five years of Portuguese progress had set in motion.

Da Gama was a determined explorer. He did not hide from storms or skirmishes, and he did not lose control of his men. Several previous ships had returned when their crews lost heart. Others fell to mutinous sailors who killed their captains and lived lives of piracy, or robbery, on the high seas. Da Gama, courageous and brutal, saw his mission through to the end. Tragically, the harshness that brought him success also set the tone for a new century of violence.

1

YOUTH AND LOYALTY

This Count, D[om] Vasco da Gama, son of Estêvão da Gama, was a man of middling stature, broad–shouldered, and fleshy, a great cavalier in his person, very resolute in his counsel, and daring in the enterprise of any action; he was unbending in his orders, and greatly to be feared in his fury, he suffered many travails and was very fair in his justice, a great execu-tor of punishments.
—Sixteenth-century historian João de Barros, reprinted in
The Career and Legend of Vasco da Gama, 1997

The exact date of Vasco da Gama's birth is unknown. Historians believe he was born in 1460 in Sines, a Portuguese seaport on the Atlantic Ocean, midway between Portugal's capital city of Lisbon (Lisboa) and the country's southernmost tip. The da Gamas were minor aris-tocrats, and Vasco's father, Estêvão da Gama, was the captain of Sines. Estêvão and his wife, Dona Isabel Sodré, had five sons. Vasco was the third, and there was at least one daughter. (At that time, female births were not recorded.)

Vasco da Gama, viceroy of India, is famous for making the first sea voyage from Europe to India. This stylized portrait, like most others, shows the great explorer as he is thought to have appeared, with reddish brown hair, a beard, and brown eyes. It originally hung in the Portuguese royal palace in the city of Goa and dates from 1524.

Although his first twenty-five years are undocumented, some scholars believe that da Gama studied in the Portuguese town of Évora. Sixteenth-century historian Gaspar Correia has written that it was at Évora that da Gama first encountered the science of astronomy, which would later serve him well on the high seas. In his twenties, da Gama may have joined the Portuguese military campaign in North Africa. At the time, it was common for sons of noble families to enter into military service. Or, his father's royal position may have given da Gama the opportunity to stay in Portugal. According to Portuguese court historian Garcia de Resende, the young da Gama "served in armadas and affairs of the sea." This suggests that he devoted time to developing the skills that eventually carried him around Africa's southern tip, which would become known later as the Cape of Good Hope, and into the Indian Ocean.

In 1492, da Gama's name suddenly appeared in the chronicles of the Portuguese king, João II. At this time, Portugal was exploring Africa's west coast. The idea behind this was twofold: King João wanted to trade with the Africans and establish Portuguese bases for the protection and supply of Portuguese ships. He needed these bases because his quest was a sea route to India, the source of the most promising trade in the world.

The Portuguese could not reach India directly by land because of the countries between Portugal and India, which controlled the trade routes. (By the mid-fourteenth

IOANNES II. LVSITANIÆ REX XIII.

Ioannes Alphonsi, et Elisabethæ filius, ortus est anno 1455. Cum 27. annū ageret Patri succedit. Ex Lusitanis Regibus nemo ullius uirtutis laude illustrior eo fuit Arma sub Patre tractauit ipse quietus regnauit nec ab aliis bello tentatus est quod in suorum beneuolentiā firmissimum habere præsidium putaretur. id ostendit Castellanorum Regina Isabella, cum suadentibus aduersus illum bellum, at nos, respondit, milites, Ioannes filios numerat. Eius Regnū memorabile apud posteros erit in primis, ob Indicæ conquisitionis initia. Nam eius auspiciis Lusitani occidentali Africæ ora perlustrata, in Austrum ita prouecti sunt, ut Bonæ Spei Promontorium, hoc est maritimam in Orientem uiam, et Ianuam aperuerint. Et inter Ethiopas quidem occiduos, quorum Regio nunc Guinea dicitur; cum Congi Regē commercia instituta, totūmque ferē illud regnum salutaribus aquis Christiano ritu Lustratum est. Ioannes Eleonoram Ferdinandi Patrui suā filiam in matrimonio habuit, Ex qua susceptum Alphonsum, cum in adolescentia extulisset, E...........................Allorii in Algarbia sanctissi. excessit ē uita...........

King João II of Portugal (1455–1495), known as the Perfect, succeeded his father, Alfonso V, in 1481. Like Portuguese leaders before him, he was eager to explore and exploit new business and trade relationships with Africa.

century, the Ottoman Turks blocked Christian travelers from using these land routes.) These countries included Italy, which had already established trade relationships with North Africa. Two Italian cities, Venice and Genoa, oversaw the entry of Eastern goods into Europe. Expensive cargoes of silks, spices, and gems shifted

11

from Arab Muslim to European Christian hands in the Egyptian city of Alexandria in North Africa. The North Africans provided the bridge to the Middle East, where merchants on camels weathered desert sandstorms. Beyond the dunes, goods arrived from across the Red Sea and the Indian Ocean, in ships that traded along the coast of India.

Luckily for the Portuguese, India was not the only source of rich trade. As they inched south along the West African coast, the Portuguese discovered gold. This was useful since Portugal was not a wealthy kingdom, and the ongoing quest for the India route was expensive. In 1492, a Portuguese ship loaded with gold failed to return home when a French vessel captured it. Sensing a threat to his plans, João II ordered the capture of all French ships at Portuguese ports. Da Gama himself led swift, successful attacks at Setúbal, Portugal, and along the Algarve coast.

Naming Portugal's King

Three years later, in 1495, João II died. Five years before his own death, João's son and heir, Prince Alfonso, had also died. (João's cousin Diogo, who was in line for the throne, had earlier attempted to seize power and had stabbed Alfonso to death.) The succession then went to the queen's brother and João's brother-in-law, Manuel (1496–1521). But João had not wanted Manuel to succeed him. While João had lived, he had tried to pass the crown to his illegitimate son, Jorge.

In order to make Jorge's birth legal, he needed the cooperation of his wife, the queen, and the pope. They refused. Unable to secure the throne for Jorge, João instead provided him with considerable power. He made Jorge the duke of Coimbra and the master of the Portuguese military.

Jorge set up a sort of counter-court to King Manuel. Although he could not make national decisions, Jorge could use his influence to limit Manuel's power. Jorge's court provided a haven for people who had been opposed to the king's succession. In 1495, Jorge wrote two letters to da Gama. In both, the duke recognized da Gama's service and loyalty. He also awarded him new rights and properties. These honors meant that da Gama became part of the counter-court of Jorge, rather than part of the court of King Manuel.

Given da Gama's loyalty to Jorge, it is surprising that the king chose him to lead Portugal's most important mission. There was no obvious reason: Da Gama was a young man who had not yet proven himself. According to some accounts, before his death, King João actually chose da Gama's father, Estêvão, to lead the expedition. If so, when Estêvão died, the right to command passed to his oldest son, Paulo. Paulo, who was unwell, may have lost this right to Vasco, under whom Paulo captained one of the voyage's four vessels. It is possible that João chose Vasco because of his success against the French.

Manuel, king of Portugal (1495–1521), was known as Manuel the Fortunate because, during his reign, Portugal's great maritime achievements were successfully completed.

Still, Manuel's choosing Vasco may have been deliberate and shrewd. By doing so, King Manuel appeared to be respecting Jorge. To grant such an honor to Vasco paid homage to Jorge. And, if the mission failed—and it seemed likely that it would—the king would not be blamed. Choosing da Gama was a clever solution to a tricky problem. King Manuel knew full well how unlikely it was that a Portuguese fleet would find a sea route, reach India, and return with its sailors alive. Any glory would be Manuel's and Portugal's. Defeat would be the fault of da Gama and Jorge.

2
THE AGE OF EXPLORATION

This [Vasco] da Gama, whose fortune it was to initiate direct European contact with the East, was a man of iron physique and surly [uncivilized] disposition . . . . For some assignments he would have been useless, but for this one he was made to order. The work lying ahead could not be accomplished by a gentle leader.

—Charles E. Nowell,
The Great Discoveries and the First Colonial Empires, 1954

Portugal is located at the southwest corner of Europe, next to Spain. For decades, the Portuguese focused their naval energies on circling Africa and reaching the East. Small and poor, Portugal seemed an unlikely contender to capture the Eastern sea route. Still, its harsh shores bred skilled, fearless sailors. In the sixteenth century (and possibly as early as the fifteenth century), the Portuguese routinely crossed the Atlantic Ocean to fish for salt cod off the Grand Banks of Canada. Because Portugal was close to Africa, its sailors did not need to pass any dangerous countries to reach the continent. England and France, both aggressive, seafaring kingdoms, lay north of the

Was hilfft der wechter in der statt/
Dem geweltigen schiff im meer sein fart
So sie Gott beyde nicht bewart.

Sailors often braced themselves against their ships, as this sixteenth-century woodcut illustrates, in order to use traditional navigational instruments such as the astrolabe, which calculated latitude, and the cross-staff, which pinpointed the position of stars and other heavenly bodies.

long, hostile Spanish coast. Italy, with its Mediterranean access and North African contacts, lacked the Atlantic training ground that bred the grittier sailors of Europe's western shoreline.

In the early fifteenth century, under King João I, Portugal fought and won several battles with Castile, a kingdom in northern Spain. The victory ended a period of tension and frequent civil war in the country, and it began one of peace. Soon after, its people focused on business, culture, and expanding their territories. Raised in prosperity, the six children of King João and Queen Philippa, who were known as the Noble Generation, inspired much of Portugal's cultural and physical growth.

The three oldest sons—Edward, Pedro, and Henry—were eager for glory and wealth. With the war over, they saw their chance to expand Portuguese power and decided that the North African coast was the perfect target for an attack. Many of its port cities were extremely wealthy because they profited from the African gold trade.

Although they were most interested in glory and riches, they also believed their attacks had a religious basis. At that time, North Africa was controlled by Muslims, followers of Islam and Muhammad rather than Christianity and Jesus Christ. This belief made them the religious enemies of the Christians in Catholic Europe. The Portuguese viewed their aggression in the light of this conflict. To attack a Muslim city was to fight for the

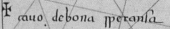

Relying on the most up-to-date geographic information available, da Gama's patron, King Manuel, provided him with maps such as this one, which depicts the coast of Africa and the Cape of Good Hope.

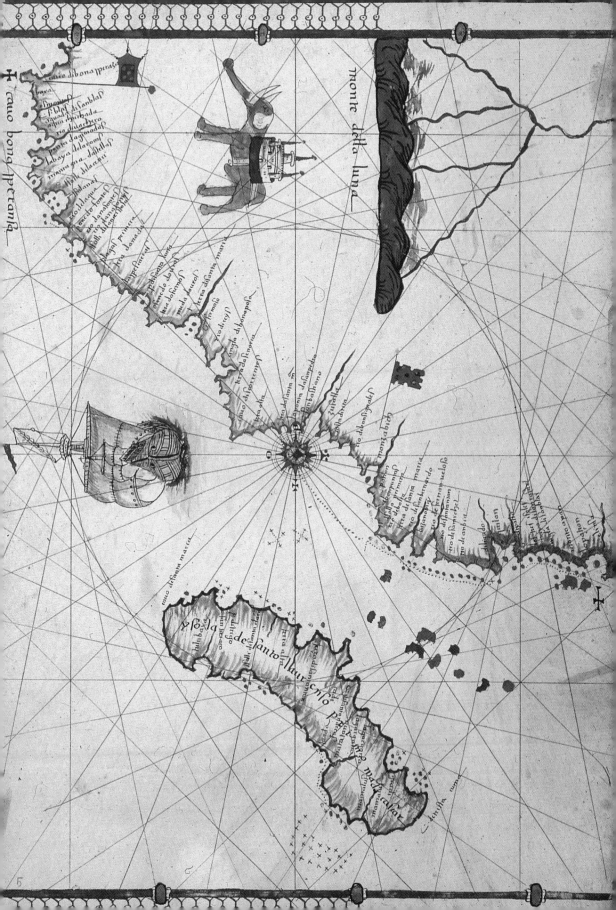

glory of the Christian world against the unbelievers, or infidels. The princes believed they would have God, and the Catholic pope, on their side.

The brothers chose the port city of Ceuta, which lay across the Strait of Gibraltar, for their attack. Rich from the gold trade and considered an easy target, Ceuta was the gateway into the Mediterranean. It would make an excellent Portuguese base on the African continent. The princes approached King João, who gave his approval for the strike.

The Victory at Ceuta

During the next year and a half, the Portuguese kingdom worked steadily, building a fleet of war vessels. On July 23, 1415, they set sail on the largest sea venture in their history. Despite storm damage and delays, the sailors persisted. They landed at Ceuta on August 20 and took the city in a day. The princes' forces killed hundreds of soldiers and civilians and lost only eight men. Delighted with his three sons, King João knighted them on the battlefield. The fleet returned home in triumph.

The capture of the Muslim city of Ceuta was Portugal's first taste of power. It provided the kingdom with victory, glory, and a renewed European foothold in the land of the Muslims. In Ceuta, the Portuguese saw lush gardens, elaborate palaces, inlaid floors, silk tapestries, finely carved furniture, and tremendous amounts of money. Most of these luxuries were destroyed in the battle. Their grandeur, however, left the Portuguese with an understanding of the importance and potential profits of increased trade. They also realized that, by doing what they saw as God's work against the infidels, they could become extremely rich.

Prince Henry the Navigator

The successful attack on Ceuta, the evidence of Eastern wealth, and the lure of adventure were intoxicating to Prince Henry. He is most often remembered as Henry the Navigator, for he launched the plan to reach India by a southern sea route, though he was never a sailor himself. Eventually, this plan culminated with the voyage of Vasco da Gama.

When Prince Henry began the quest for a southern route to India, few people believed such a voyage was possible. For generations, Portuguese sailors had known and avoided the seas south of the Canary Islands. This was not cowardice; it was common sense. These men had no intention of losing their lives on missions that their grandfathers' grandfathers had known to be voyages of certain death.

In the fifteenth century, many Europeans believed that the heat of the sun made the sea boil near the equator. They thought that huge sea monsters lived in the southern waters. Sightings of giant whales, dolphins, huge conger eels, and mammoth forty-foot squid spawned stories of ships grasped by tentacles and dragged into the deep sea.

This portrait of Portugal's Prince Henry dates from the sixteenth century. He was known as Henry the Navigator, and it was his vision and perseverance, not his sailing ability, that led his country into the age of exploration.

The ocean off the arid Sahara coast did appear to boil because the sea was unusually shallow well out from land. Even worse, the dark red dust that blew west off the desert wafted a sinister haze over the water, convincing some sailors that the water was filled with blood. Believed to be the work of Satan, this image unnerved the few sailors who saw it.

Prince Henry knew these fears to be unfounded because he had read ancient accounts of successful voyages around the tip of Africa. He knew that at least one fleet had circled the continent. During the Twenty-sixth Dynasty in Egypt (663–525 BC), the Egyptian king, Pharaoh Necho II, had hired a group of Phoenician sailors to circumnavigate Africa. The voyage, which took more than three years, was fortified with supplies from land. The crews would stop to plant and harvest crops in the fertile African soil. Once reprovisioned, they would continue their voyage. Because Prince Henry knew it was possible to sail safely down the western coast of Africa, he decided to send a ship past the Canary Islands.

Prince Henry proposed his plans, fortified by literary proof, to his father and the royal court. Like all voyages in those years, any exploration, no matter how dangerous, was deemed worthy because it provided an opportunity for European Catholics to convert non-Christians.

During the Middle Ages, sailors believed the ocean was teeming with sea monsters. Little did they know that the most perilous danger of long sea adventures would be malnutrition—causing most of da Gama's crew, some 115 men, to die of scurvy and starvation.

In 1419, Prince Henry sent a crew of fishermen and merchant sailors south along the African coastline. His men refused to pass Cape Bojador (just south of the Canary Islands, approximately 1,000 miles south of Lisbon). They harbored superstitions that proved stronger than the prince's royal orders. Instead of continuing, the crew attacked the ships of several Arab merchants. These attacks amassed enough wealth for Prince Henry to fund a second voyage. In the 1420s, his captains discovered uninhabited islands to the west, which they named the Madeira Islands.

The Madeiras were wooded and fertile, so Prince Henry sent people to settle on them. His colonists grew sugarcane, picked grapes for wine, and cut wood for timber. The venture provided him with more wealth and a useful port.

By 1433, after more than a dozen ships failed to pass Cape Bojador, Prince Henry gave Captain Gil Eanes an unconditional order to sail beyond it. To calm the fears of the sailors, Eanes tried a new route. Rather than sailing south along the coast, he headed west to the Canaries and then south. When he calculated that his ship was fifty miles past the cape, he turned east. To his surprise and relief, the sea south of Bojador was calm and quiet. An unremarkable coastline came in sight. Once ashore, the explorers found plants and the footprints of men and camels. Finally, the Portuguese age of exploration had begun.

The Cape of Good Hope

King João's death in 1433 sparked a power struggle among his sons for Portugal's throne. Prince Henry, however, had no personal interest in the crown but nevertheless spent the next few years embroiled in political affairs.

During this time, his men focused on improving the design of their ships. Their square-sailed rigs, built for steady winds, struggled against the unpredictable gusts off the African coast. Arabian ships, designed mainly for the currents and seas of their usual trade routes, used only triangular sails. This design enabled their captains to steer their vessels more easily in heavy winds. The Arabian vessels' shallow hulls allowed them to hug the shore, skim into bays, and avoid shoals (sandbanks). The deep hulls of the Portuguese ships frequently ran aground in shallow waters.

The Portuguese changed their ships' design and experimented by blending Arabian innovation with their own experience. The result was a new vessel: the caravel. Fast and light, the caravel used a lateen rig with a triangular sail capable of heading into the wind.

Da Gama's 1497–1498 journey around Africa to India marked the longest ocean voyage ever taken at the time. In addition to carrying the best supplies of the day, the ships were outfitted with stone markers and wooden crosses to claim new lands in the name of Portugal and the Roman Catholic Church.

DEMONSTRAÇÃO DA I

Mangate

N. Sra da Esperanca.

Vaypim

Pexo da pimenta

N.S. da Graça

Bazar

S. Agostinho

Anunciada

Leiturolay

Cais

Camera

Misericordia

Sé

Casa do Povo

Cais

Hospital

This is a seventeenth-century city layout of the Portuguese
quarter of Cochin, the port city on India's southern coast
where the Portuguese established their first trading outpost.

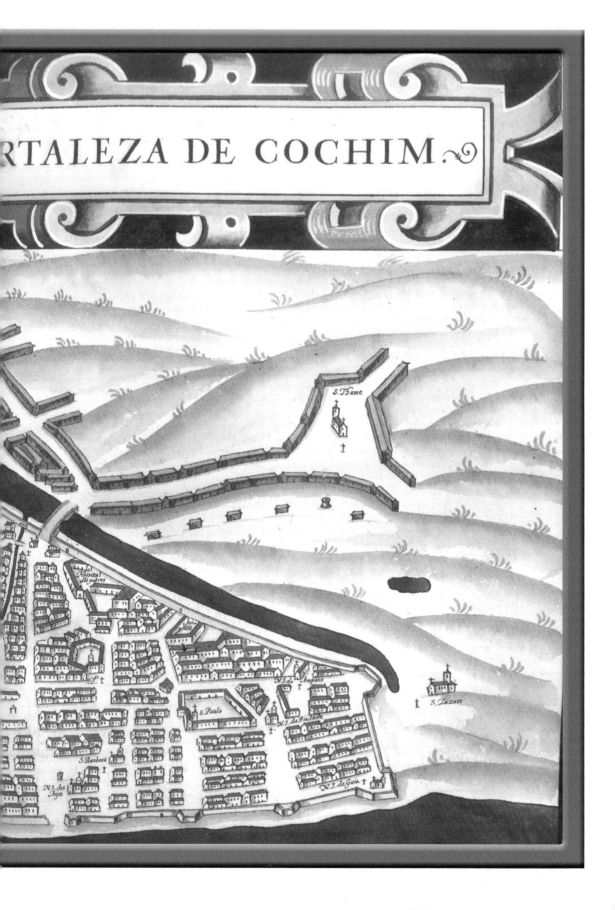

By the 1440s, Prince Henry was urging his sailors to head farther south. Portugal's holdings along the coast and in the West African islands expanded greatly. Success made the sailors bold. They began taking captives, kidnappings that they justified on the basis of their religious beliefs. At the time, many European Catholics truly believed that converting people to Christianity saved them from eternal damnation. The Portuguese converted their captives, then sold them as slaves. The profits from this slave trade increased funds for exploration and future raids. In 1445, more than two dozen ships sailed from Portugal, all seeking easy money from the new slave trade.

Not surprisingly, people along the West African coast became wary of white men traveling by sea. In 1446, Nuno Tristão, a Portuguese sailor, anchored at the mouth of the Gambia River. When he and his crew rowed a small boat upriver into the jungle, the area looked like impenetrable wilderness. They were completely unprepared for the sudden flurry of poisonous arrows that killed four men and wounded fourteen. The five survivors sailed home to report the first Portuguese defeat at West African hands.

Despite this attack and others like it, the Portuguese had been negotiating trade agreements with African rulers more frequently and to one another's mutual benefit. When Prince Henry died in 1460, his nephew Alfonso, now king of Portugal, resumed the quest. When Alfonso's son, João II, was appointed to the throne in August of 1481, he spent his first five years pressing his men farther down the African coast. By 1486, he had bases in the areas now known as Ghana, Angola, and Zaire.

The following year, King João II sent out an expedition of three ships, commanded by Bartolomeu de Novais Dias, another seasoned Portuguese explorer, with orders to reach the tip of the African continent. Three months into the voyage, the ships reached the twenty-ninth parallel, only a few degrees north of their goal. Then, the weather turned. Dias could not fight the wind. He decided to leave the supply ship behind and head west. His plan was to duck around the weather and then return to land.

After two weeks, the seas improved. To his surprise, the land now ran in an east-west, rather than a north-south, direction. He followed the south-facing coast until it curved northeast. Dias had finally rounded the bottom of the African continent, a place he named Cabo Tormentoso, or the Cape of Storms, a name later rejected by the king as he felt it was too dreary. (The original name was recalled as a prophecy in 1500 when Dias was drowned there during a storm.)

By then, Dias's men had had enough. The tireless leader argued that endless glory lay ahead, but his men were adamant. They wanted to go home. Realizing that they would not yield, a disappointed Dias erected a cross and a pillar where he had landed on the cape and sailed back to Lisbon. King João was elated; to him the voyage was a huge victory. He renamed the tip of Africa the Cape of Good Hope, in anticipation of the great fortune that would soon be Portugal's.

The Appointment

In the years following Dias's trip around the tip of Africa, King João II focused his attention on his African bases. He wanted Portuguese merchants to have safe ports. They would need to rest and reprovision between the legs of their long voyages. During this period, the Portuguese explored the surrounding ocean aggressively. This may be when they first became aware of Brazil, which, officially, Pedro Álvares Cabral reached more than a decade later, in 1500. Due to their legendary secrecy, it is impossible to determine exactly what they understood regarding the boundaries of the Atlantic Ocean. Portuguese rutters, or secret sailing manuals, were among the most closely guarded documents in the world. The Portuguese were fiercely protective of their knowledge, especially since it gave them an edge over the rest of Europe.

When Dias returned from the Cape of Good Hope in 1488, an experienced Genoese sailor, Christopher Columbus, was struggling to raise money for an expedition across the Atlantic to the west. Columbus was married to a

The great Italian explorer Christopher Columbus also set out to "discover" India—for Spain, not Portugal—but ended up in the Caribbean, in a group of islands he believed bordered the coast of Asia.

Portuguese aristocrat named Felipa Perestrello e Moniz. He knew the islands of Madeira, the Azores, and some of the African coastline. Columbus believed that the land across the Atlantic Ocean was Asia, and he proposed a voyage there to the councillors of João II. The councillors, however, dismissed the proposal on the grounds that the king did not fund the voyages of independent explorers. Because of Dias's achievement, the Portuguese expected to reach India by sailing east; they did not need Columbus or his extensive knowledge of the Atlantic Ocean.

Columbus eventually found funding in Spain in 1492. He sailed to what he believed to be Asia and returned with evidence such as gold, amber, native plants, and native people that he called Indians. Meanwhile, the Portuguese prepared for a more extensive expedition. In 1495, before they completed the journey, João, still in his late thirties, died of an unknown disease. The next king of Portugal was Manuel, who, in early 1497, chose Vasco da Gama to lead the voyage to India.

3

THE VOYAGE

At daybreak of Thursday the 16th of November, having careened our ships and taken in woods we set sail. At that time we did not know how far we might be abaft [behind] the Cape of Good Hope . . . We therefore stood out towards S.S.W., and late on Saturday [November 18] we beheld the Cape. On that same day we again stood out to sea, returning to the land in the course of the night. On Sunday morning, November 19, we once more made for the Cape, but were again unable to round it.
—Excerpt from the logbooks of Vasco da Gama, 1497

Vasco da Gama set out for India with four ships. Two of these, the *São Gabriel* and the *São Rafael*, were carracks. Unlike the exploratory caravels, the carracks were big galleons with square-rigged sails and large cargo holds. Both of them carried twenty cannons each. The third vessel, named the *São Miguel* but called the *Bérrio*, was a caravel. Finally, there was a supply ship that carried food to last the entire expedition for three years. Da Gama commanded from the *São Gabriel*. One of da Gama's brothers, Paulo, captained the *São Rafael*, and Nicolão Coelho sailed the *Bérrio*.

Da Gama's flagship, the *São Gabriel*, was part of a fleet of four ships that included the *São Rafael* and the *Bérrio*. They carried twenty bombards, or medieval cannons, each which had the capacity to hurl large stone balls at any potential enemy.

The crew included Fernão Martins, who was fluent in Arabic, since da Gama would need an interpreter. Also along for the ride, aboard the *São Rafael*, was Álvaro Velho, the sailor credited for the journal that provides the most thorough first-person account of the voyage.

Around the Cape

The fleet set sail on July 8, 1497, passed the Canary Islands a week later, and in relatively short time sighted the coast, south of Cape Bojador. On July 17, the ships were separated in a deep fog, but by July 26, they had all reached the Cape Verde Islands. They sailed on to Santiago Island, stopped to reprovision, and continued their voyage south. Da Gama followed the lead of Dias in sailing west and then south to avoid the treacherous coastal winds, calculating with great precision. After three months, da Gama and his crew entered a South African waterway that they named the Bay of St. Helena, thirty miles north of the Cape of Good Hope.

This was an astounding accomplishment. There are no landmarks on the open ocean. In the years leading up to da Gama's voyage, the Portuguese had reached an extraordinary level of navigational skill. Using the charts of previous voyages and the constellations in the night sky, they were able to find known areas and chart the discoveries of new places. Da Gama's success was the end product of an organized, long-term plan.

Da Gama determined that the bay would provide a safe harbor and anchored there on November 8. The crew spent eight days resting, mending the sails, and gathering fresh provisions. The local people seemed amiable. Velho noted that they ate seal and deer meat and kept dogs. Da Gama traded with them merely for the experience and got little more than shells (cowrie shells were used as currency in parts of the West African coast) in return.

A sailor named Fernão Veloso went ashore and ate with the local people. After the meal, he wanted to see their homes, but they told him to go back to his ship. Thwarted, Veloso called out to his comrades for a ride. The men who came to collect him sailed into shore at a speed that may have seemed threatening. Alarmed, the Africans threw several spears, wounding da Gama and three of his crewmen.

According to Velho, the Portuguese had been too trusting. He also regretted that they were not better armed. Given Velho's perspective, it is unclear whether the Africans expected violence. Without detailed information, one cannot judge whether they had reason to attack. Da Gama, historians have noted, was a man of action, not a diplomat capable of sensitive, cross-cultural communication. What occurred at the Bay of St. Helena was the first in a long chain of incidents that aggravated his increasingly suspicious mind.

Among the important contributions to Vasco da Gama's successful ocean crossing were the sky charts and calculation tables given to him by Abraham Zacuto, a Jewish astronomer and mathematician who had fled to Portugal from Spain in 1492 to avoid religious persecution.

Mossel Bay

Da Gama set sail from the Bay of St. Helena on November 16. Two days later, a lookout saw land. The vessels were sailing into a hard wind, and it took them until noon on November 22 to clear the point.

Three days later, they reached the Bay of São Brás, or Mossel Bay. Once docked, da Gama ordered his men to remove the contents of the cumbersome supply ship before he had it destroyed. Without it, the remaining ships could travel much faster.

After six days, a large group of men appeared on the beach. Da Gama traded with them for a large ox, which he killed to feed his crew. At one point, the Africans played music and danced on the beach while the Portuguese played their trumpets and danced on board their ships. Despite this show of goodwill, there was some confusion regarding a second ox, which ended with the Portuguese firing two cannon shots. When they left on December 5, the sailors built a pillar and a tall cross made from the mizzenmast of the burned supply ship and erected them on the bluff over the water. As they sailed out, they saw a dozen people destroying the cross.

By December 16, da Gama passed the end mark of Dias's expedition. The crew sighted the pillar Dias had erected on the shore and knew they were now in unexplored territory.

The land was beautiful. Trees grew thick and tall. Cattle roamed the fields. The fleet then reached the Inharrime River region.

The local people were Bantu. Their copper ornaments and their friendliness led da Gama and his men to name their river the Rio de Cobre (River of Copper) and their land the Terra da Boa-Gente (Land of the Good People).

From Inharrime, they headed north to the Zambezi River, where they stopped again. Many of the sailors had scurvy, a disease in which the feet, hands, and gums swell painfully. Caused by a lack of vitamin C, scurvy was common among those at sea for long periods. At the Zambezi, they enjoyed another friendly reception. The locals rowed out with fresh water. They were polite but unimpressed by da Gama's trinkets. According to Velho, one wore a cap of green satin and another a hat with silk-embroidered tassels. They claimed that they traded frequently with other light-skinned sea merchants who carried more valuable goods such as gold and copper. Da Gama concluded that he must be near the trade routes of the East. When he left on February 24, he erected a pillar in what he had named the Rio de Bons Sinais, or the River of Good Omens.

The East African Coast

On March 1, 1498, da Gama anchored his fleet off Mozambique Island, a major African trade center. The local sultan (leader) rowed out to visit the Portuguese fleet, and da Gama presented him with gifts of coral. Disappointed by the offering, the sultan refused it. Da Gama realized that his merchandise might not appeal to Eastern traders. According to Velho, the Mozambicans spoke Arabic and wore fine linen. They told da Gama that they traded with white Muslims for gold, silver, cloves, pepper, rubies, and seed pearls.

The Mozambicans were suspicious of the Portuguese's lack of fine goods. If the Portuguese were not in East Africa to trade, they thought, perhaps they were pirates. Another source of discomfort was the Portuguese's religious secrecy (which they thought would avoid religious hostility). Despite this precaution, it was probably obvious to the sultan that the sailors were not Muslims. Toward the end of their stay, they celebrated mass on an island away from the city. Along the way, the armed crews of some local boats asked them to return to port, but da Gama refused. Suddenly, he ordered his men to fire.

Either this incident or the pilots da Gama had hired alerted the sultan that the Portuguese were Christians. Soon after his arrival, da Gama had asked the sultan for two pilots. Da Gama's charts ran out where Dias's voyage ended. He had had good luck afterward, as the Mozambicans were skilled sailors, but he saw no point in sailing blindly. Da Gama paid the pilots well but insisted that one remain on board at all times, almost as a hostage.

It is unclear whether the sultan was most disturbed by the sailors' Christianity, their attempts to hide it, their attack on his men, or da Gama's detainment of the pilots. Velho

Among the tactics for Vasco da Gama's successful voyage was the fact that he hired experienced Arab seamen to navigate his fleet across the Arabian Sea—a journey of more than twenty days—to the shores of India, waters that were previously unknown to European sailors.

wrote with conviction that once the sultan knew they were Christians, he became determined to capture and kill them. Historically, this information is mere conjecture. Ignoring the usual customs of departure, such as attending a traditional mass, the Portuguese sailed out of Mozambique.

Through the fluent Arabic of Fernão Martins, da Gama learned that there were many Christian cities north of Mozambique. At the time, da Gama held the mistaken belief that all Indians were Christians (only some people in the south of India were Christian at the time). Martins's news reassured da Gama, who imagined he was entering Christian territory and headed north.

However, the winds off the coast were cruel. For more than two weeks, his crew fought the weather. Finally, da Gama returned to replenish his supplies. The sultan sent a man to make peace with the Portuguese, but he was unsuccessful. That night, da Gama's crew rowed into shore to find freshwater. The following evening, twenty armed men surrounded its source. Da Gama fired at them and took all the water he wanted. Relations grew very hostile. Always hot-tempered, da Gama decided to make an example of the situation. He returned to the beach, fired again, killed two men, captured two boats, and took several prisoners. On March 29, the Portuguese sailed out of Mozambique for good.

Mombasa

On April 1, the fleet stopped at a group of islands, which they misidentified as the mainland. When da Gama discovered one of the pilots was either mistaken or lying, he had him flogged (beaten). They then set forth for the island of Kilwa, which the pilots claimed, incorrectly again, was settled by Christians. Plagued by uncooperative winds, da Gama instead headed north in hope of reaching the town of Mombasa. A few days later, the *São Rafael* ran aground on a shoal. When the tide rose to free it, two local people sailed out to them on boats loaded with oranges. Delighted by the gift, the Portuguese felt that their luck had changed. They sailed past Zanzibar and Pemba.

On April 7, they arrived at Mombasa. It was here, according to the pilots, that there were two communities: one Muslim and one Christian. The Christians, who lived in a separate quarter and ruled themselves, welcomed them.

Tense and extremely wary, da Gama anchored outside the port. When a boat carrying 100 men rowed out to the *São Gabriel*, da Gama allowed only five on board. The Mombasans might have been gauging the strength of his crew. One hundred men, it was estimated, could easily try to seize a ship. The meeting was cordial, but da Gama remained tense. The sultan of Mombasa then sent a gift of sheep and fruit. Not to answer would be an insult, so da Gama sent two men into port. They visited the town and the homes of two Christian merchants and returned with presents of ginger, pepper, and cloves. According to the sultan, da Gama was welcome to load his ship with these treasures if he, too, would enter the port.

Da Gama considered his options. On one hand, his men were unwell. They needed fresh food and rest. The next day was Palm Sunday. Anchored off a town they believed to be partially Christian, the men wanted to attend mass. Still, da Gama suspected a trap. On the other hand, with a full cargo of valuable spices, he could easily sail home. His orders from King Manuel were to round the Cape of Good Hope and open the Eastern trade route. This implied, but did not stipulate, that he reach

Because the luxurious spices and gems of the East were handled exclusively by Muslim merchants before 1498, Arabs were understandably threatened by the presence of European traders who could then gain access to the valuable goods and gain great profits.

the shores of India. If he filled his holds now, he could spare his men the probable horror of crossing the Indian Ocean. Given the examples he had seen, the profit would be enormous.

By April 10, a still undecided da Gama witnessed a strange incident that has been told in two different ways. In one version of this story, seeing that the Portuguese fleet did not intend to enter the city, the Muslims on board decided to return to shore. As they passed the prow (front) of da Gama's ship, the Mozambican pilots flung themselves from the vessel's sides and swam for the Muslim boat. In another version, da Gama did decide to enter port. Due to the low tide, the *São Gabriel* was slightly aground. When the crew drew anchor, the vessel did not move. The other two ships saw the predicament and dropped anchor again. Unaware of the problem, the few Mombasans aboard, as well as the Mozambican pilots, saw the ships halt, believed the action revealed their treachery, and dove into the sea.

Whatever happened, da Gama was extremely suspicious. He tortured the two remaining Muslims. When he dropped hot oil on their skin, they "confessed." It is impossible to know if what they had told him was the truth, or what they felt da Gama wanted to hear. They told da Gama that the sultan intended to capture the Portuguese fleet. The Muslims claimed that the sultan of Mombasa wanted to avenge da Gama's actions at Mozambique. That night, several Mombasans rowed out to the Portuguese ships and tried to cut their anchor lines, presumably hoping that the vessels would either drift out to sea or sink. The Portuguese prevented their actions, but it was clear they had to leave. Pilotless, da Gama sailed north.

Malindi

A short distance from the Island of Mombasa, da Gama's fleet captured a merchant ship carrying a rich cargo of gold and silver. Da Gama looted the hold and imprisoned the elderly merchant, his wife, and the seventeen crew members, none of whom were pilots. They recommended that da Gama search for a pilot at Malindi, the next port. Malindi was another large trading island, about sixty miles away. According to some of da Gama's captives, there were four Christian or Indian ships there.

The sultan of Malindi had heard of da Gama, his crew's history at Mombasa, and the capture of the merchant ship. When the Portuguese fleet arrived, it was not greeted. Finally, da Gama sent the merchant to offer greetings to the sultan. The merchant returned with gifts, the promise of pilots, and an invitation to the palace, but da Gama refused to go ashore. He politely requested that the sultan meet him instead. Finally, the two men sat together in one of da Gama's rowboats. The meeting went well. As it turned out, the sultans of Malindi and Mombasa loathed each other. Da Gama fired his cannons in honor of the sultan of Malindi and released his remaining Muslim prisoners. This action was both gracious and shrewd. The sultan immediately embraced da Gama's point of view. Two Portuguese sailors went ashore to visit the royal palaces, while the sultan left two men, one of whom was his son, with da Gama. This exchange of hostages reassured the Portuguese.

Da Gama was now focused on finding a pilot. Eventually, with the help of the sultan, he approached a Hindu from the Indian region of Gujarat, known in Portuguese as Malemo Cana or Malemo Canaca. This is a version of the title "master astronomer." Although his true identity is uncertain, the man was an able navigator.

Calicut, India

That spring, da Gama sailed out of Malindi across the Indian Ocean toward the city of Calicut in India. On May 18, the lookout sighted a mountain range, the Western Ghats, a chain of highlands that follows the western edge of the Indian subcontinent.

Two days later, the fleet anchored north of Calicut, on the Malabar coast of India. That night, locals sailed out to greet the crew, and da Gama explained his business in Calicut. The Indians agreed to take a Portuguese sailor ashore with them the next morning.

On May 21, this man (possibly the *degredado*, or convict-exile, João Nunes) became the first Portuguese person to set foot in India. Once ashore, he met two North African merchants who spoke both Castilian Spanish and Genoese Italian, and who reportedly said, "May the devil take you! What brought you here?" Announcing the Portuguese quest for spices and Christians, the response was that not only were there Christians but also rubies and emeralds enough to gather in baskets!

Feeling unusually optimistic, da Gama sent a message to the zamorin, or king of Calicut, who was not a Christian but a Hindu. The king was away, but he sent a welcoming message and a pilot to guide them to a more accommodating port.

On May 28, the zamorin returned and sent an elaborate entourage to escort da Gama to the palace. Before the group reached the city, however, they stopped at a church. The priests sprinkled the sailors with holy water and ashes. Velho noticed that the saints painted on the walls did not appear Christian since all wore diadems (crowns), some had very large teeth, and most had four or six arms. What da Gama thought was a church was probably a Hindu temple of Vaishnavas, worshipers of the Hindu god Vishnu.

Curious crowds mobbed da Gama's crew. At one point, the escort dispersed the people forcibly. Finally, just before dusk, they

When Vasco da Gama visited the zamorin of Calicut, the ruler was doubtful of the explanation da Gama had given for his journey. Even so, he gave the captain-major a letter for the Portuguese king written on a palm leaf that stated his pleasure at the sailors' arrival.

arrived at the palace. Once there, they were welcomed by a holy man who embraced da Gama and immediately took him to the lavish chamber where he held court. The zamorin lay on a cushioned dais draped with fine velvets, chewing betel leaves, which he kept nearby in a golden vat. A canopy hung above his head. He greeted da Gama with his palms pressed together and his arms raised. According to his log, da Gama "saluted in the manner of the country: by putting his hands together, then raising them towards

Heaven, as is done by Christians when addressing God, and immediately afterwards opening them and quickly shutting his fists." The zamorin offered fruit to the Portuguese and then laughed heartily at the foreign way in which they ate.

In contrast to his crew, da Gama's knowledge of proper etiquette was impressive. He knew that before speaking to the zamorin, one must bend forward and hold one hand in front of one's mouth. When da Gama refused to explain his mission in front of the courtiers, the zamorin agreed to meet with him privately.

Through Fernão Martins's translation, da Gama described his voyage as a mission to form alliances with other Christian kingdoms. He explained that the Portuguese ruler, King Manuel, governed many lands and possessed much wealth and did not seek the riches of other kingdoms. King Manuel had ordered da Gama to sail to India to befriend such important rulers as the zamorin of Calicut. Da Gama also said that if he were to fail, King Manuel would cut off his head.

Even though he had no way of knowing that it was mostly lies, the zamorin liked da Gama's presentation. He offered the Portuguese food and lodging. At da Gama's insistence, he arranged for the visitors to sleep away from both the Muslim and the Hindu (which da Gama still believed were Christian) quarters in the city.

After reaching India in 1498, da Gama obtained an audience with the king, or zamorin, of Calicut. The explorer announced his good intentions and falsely claimed that he would be beheaded if the king did not befriend him.

India was experiencing its monsoon season, and many roads were flooded. Subsequently, da Gama ordered his men to carry him through the wet streets. One of the Muslim guides offered da Gama a horse. He accepted, but when he found that he had to ride bareback, he declined. Finally, his crew, now exhausted, reached their lodgings. Inside, there was a bed for da Gama and several of their trunks of goods intended as gifts for the zamorin, which had been sent ahead. Even though da Gama and his crew felt secure, everything was about to fall apart.

Negotiations

The Portuguese had nothing to offer a wealthy Eastern ruler. The trinkets they had traded in Africa (where trade was limited and there were few or no manufactured goods) looked common in India. The zamorin's men examined the gifts and laughed in amusement. According to Velho, the objects included "twelve pieces of striped cloth, four scarlet hoods, six hats, four strings of coral, a case of six wash-hand basins, a case of sugar, two casks of oil, and two of honey." Da Gama told them that the few items he had to offer were his own. He was an ambassador, not a merchant, and he wasn't rich. He claimed that his poverty was unrelated to the wealth of Portugal's king. The zamorin's men told him that they would not take his gifts to the zamorin, nor would they allow him to present them.

Meanwhile, the zamorin summoned da Gama and asked him why he had come with such useless goods. It was impossible for the zamorin to believe that a kingdom as rich as Portugal would send an ambassador with trinkets in an effort to increase trade between peoples. The zamorin could not take da Gama seriously, either as an ally or as a trader. He told da Gama to sell his merchandise at the local market instead, but the local merchants also dismissed the goods and considered them worthless.

Da Gama's next idea was to build a large cargo of spices from trading in small amounts. To this end, he sent his men ashore to trade, but the exchange rate for the Portuguese goods remained low. All in all, da Gama amassed small samples of cloves, cinnamon, and a few gems. In an attempt to repair relations with the zamorin, da Gama sent his scribe, Diogo Dias, with some gifts. The zamorin remained uninterested in the Portuguese. His concern was only that da Gama not sail out of Calicut without paying port duties (taxes). Meanwhile, a local man informed the Portuguese that their lives were in danger and described a plot to murder da Gama. At this, da Gama decided to get his men and his remaining goods back on board his ships. The men still ashore could not leave without the zamorin's agreement, nor could da Gama reload his remaining cargo.

The ancient city of Calicut, shown in this woven wall hanging, was a flourishing port and trading center when Vasco da Gama landed there in 1498. Famed for its cotton weaving, the city's name eventually lent itself to the English word "calico," which originally meant "cloth from Calicut."

On August 19, twenty-five men rowed a boat out to the *São Gabriel*. Da Gama captured eighteen of them. Then he sent a message to the zamorin offering to exchange the hostages for his own men. After four days without an answer, he decided to set sail, but foul winds held him off of the coast of Calicut. On August 26, a boat brought a message from the zamorin, claiming that he wanted to negotiate. Concerned that any delay would give the zamorin enough time to gather naval reinforcements, da Gama demanded his men back at once.

The zamorin sent Dias, who was still ashore, to da Gama with the message that he knew nothing about these bad feelings and that he blamed corrupt officials. The zamorin said he would like to become an ally of King Manuel. Dias transcribed this letter from the zamorin to the king: "Vasco da Gama, hidalgo [gentleman] of your household, came to my land, and I rejoiced at that. In my land, there is much cinnamon, and much cloves and ginger and pepper and many precious stones. And what I want from your land is gold and silver and coral and scarlet."

At this, da Gama released some hostages and promised to release the others when the Portuguese goods were returned to him. The zamorin tried to satisfy all of da Gama's demands, but the explorer abruptly changed his mind. Announcing that he would rather take the hostages, he instead fled from India on August 29 with a sampling of Indian goods and twelve captives.

The medieval text featured on this page is a folio from an Arabic version of Dioscorides' *De Materia Medica*. It discusses the medicinal (healing) properties of cinnamon, a spice much valued during the Middle Ages.

The Journey Home

The adventure in India continued. By September 10, the fleet was only one port north of Calicut. Nine days later, they reached the Anjedive Islands south of Goa. Here, the local people welcomed them with food and cinnamon. Forever suspicious, da Gama soon sighted eight boats on the horizon. The islanders had detained da Gama's fleet while a Calicut fleet approached.

The Portuguese continued sailing north and stopped on yet another island. Here, the worshipers at a ruined church warned them that pirates used the port as a frequent stopping place. When two ships approached, the Portuguese fired without hesitation, scaring off what may have been corsairs (pirates). At the next port, they met a spy who tried, but failed, to entrap them. (He was hideously flogged for his treachery. Still on board when they sailed, the spy later made peace with da Gama. Back in Portugal, he converted to Christianity and called himself Gaspar da Gama after his "godfather," Vasco.)

In their many attempts to trade with the people and rulers of Africa and India, the Portuguese were sometimes frustrated by their own lack of goods and diplomatic skills, and by their expectation of deceit. They often felt persecuted, powerless, and poor. As a result, they resorted to an arena in which they were clearly superior: naval firepower. As his voyage progressed, da Gama reacted to complex situations with violence. One of his final acts was to burn a captured boat that he refused to sell back to its owner for any amount of money.

On October 5, 1498, the Portuguese finally set sail for the West but were delayed by bad weather. The crossing that had taken three weeks from Africa to India took more than three months in the opposite direction. Conditions on board were horrible. Thirty men died of scurvy. Had the situation lasted just two more weeks, the fleet might not have made it.

They reached Mogadishu on January 2, 1499. Several days later, they secured their vessels at Malindi, where the sultan sent them freshwater, supplies, and enough oranges to counter the deteriorating effects of scurvy.

The fleet set out again, passing Mombasa and reaching the shoals where, nine months earlier, the *São Rafael* had run aground. Judging his crew too shorthanded to man three ships, da Gama ordered them to unload and burn the *São Rafael*. They sailed on past Zanzibar and Mozambique. In early March, they reached Mossel Bay, where they caught and salted (preserved) anchovies,

King Manuel was so satisfied with the results of Vasco da Gama's voyage that he inaccurately took to calling himself Lord of Guinea and of the Conquest, Navigation, and Commerce of Ethiopia, Arabia, Persia, and India. This painting depicts da Gama presenting King Manuel with treasures from India.

seals, and penguins for the journey up the west coast. The stretch from the Cape of Good Hope to the island of Santiago took twenty-seven days. Somewhere off West Africa, storms separated the two ships. The *Bérrio* was home by July 10, almost exactly two years after its departure. The *São Gabriel* reached Lisbon in August, and da Gama, who stopped in the Azores to bury his brother Paulo, who had died on the journey, arrived a few weeks later.

King Manuel was delighted. He saw clearly that despite their small cargo, unimaginable wealth lay in wait—a wealth that Portugal could control. No other European country had either the knowledge or the experience to make the journey. King Manuel greeted da Gama with honor and provided him with a large income. The king named him admiral of India and paraded him proudly through the streets of Lisbon.

4

PORTUGAL CHANGES THE WORLD

[There was] a storm and a rain of iron and stone projectiles, which caused very great destruction, in which many people died as well. When night fell, to speed things up, and for greater terror, he [da Gama] had the heads, hands and feet of the hanged men cut off, and put on a boat with a letter, in which he said that if those men, though they were not the same who had been responsible for the death of the Portuguese, and only on account of being relatives of the residents, had received that punishment, the authors of that treachery could await a manner of death that was even more cruel.
—João de Barros, *Décadas da Ásia*, 1552

D a Gama did not "discover" the country of India. It had already existed for thousands of years. Rather, he established the possibility of a trade route that skipped most other merchants between Spain and Africa. Portugal now had almost exclusive access to such invaluable spices as ginger, pepper, cinnamon, and cloves. Prior to da Gama's discovery, Europeans had obtained goods from merchants at the end of a long chain of traders, each of whom increased the price of their wares to cover their own

VASCO DE GAMA

Because of his daring and courageous attitude, Vasco da Gama, despite his brutality, is still revered as a national hero by Portugal. In 1998, the Portuguese celebrated the 500th anniversary of his first voyage to India.

Gros fecit

expenses. According to Velho, spice growers delivered their harvested goods to trading centers like Calicut. From there, the bundles journeyed for weeks or months to Jeddah in Arabia, where the grand sultan taxed them. After, they crossed the Red Sea and stopped in the city of Tuuz, near Mount Sinai. Here again, merchants were forced to pay duties (taxes).

Finally, the merchants traveled on land, by camel, to Egypt's city of Cairo. This leg of the trip was very hazardous, as the desert was filled with bandits. From Cairo, they were sent down the Nile River to Rosetta and were taxed once more. Then they were loaded back onto camels for the one-day trip to Alexandria, the ancient city and thriving marketplace named for the Greek leader Alexander the Great. The city, known for its abundant trading, provided the bridge between Africa and Europe. There, merchant galleys from Italian cities such as Genoa and Venice arrived with bags of coins and left with trucks of spices. Back in Europe, they sold these spices at exorbitant rates. Thanks to da Gama, King Manuel could now bypass these expensive steps. He could pay low prices at Calicut for goods that in Europe he could mark up more than 1,000 percent.

To flood the European market with luxury items from the East was a bold idea. Underselling long-standing trade arrangements would antagonize many powerful countries. Still, for King Manuel, the benefits outweighed the risks. While da Gama recovered from his arduous, two-year voyage, the king organized a second, larger fleet under the command of Pedro Álvares Cabral (1467–1520). Da Gama recommended that they set sail in winter or early spring. Based on the time it would take to travel down and then up the coast of Africa, da Gama estimated that this schedule would position the ships to take full advantage of the late-summer monsoon season. He assumed that the strong monsoon winds would push the ships across the Indian Ocean and then lessen, leaving the traders with fair weather for business in India.

New Conflicts

Cabral sailed on March 9, 1500, with thirteen ships and 1,500 men. He lost one ship near the Cape Verde Islands, sent another back after "discovering" Brazil, and lost four more rounding the cape. Another, under the command of Diogo Dias, abandoned the fleet, sailing to Madagascar and then north toward the Red Sea. The remaining ships put in at the Muslim port of Kilwa, where relations were awkward. They moved on and then were welcomed at Malindi. As he had done for da Gama, the sultan of Malindi provided Cabral with another pilot.

The crossing of the Indian Ocean took one month. Cabral arrived in Calicut in mid-September with his six remaining ships. The former zamorin of Calicut had died since da Gama's departure. Cabral approached

67

Even after roughly 100 years since its adaptation in the Portuguese port town Lagos, the caravel was a sturdy, speedy ship that was among the most popular with fifteenth- and sixteenth-century sailors.

the new zamorin with a request for hostages. Only then, he said, would he step on land. The zamorin met Cabral and was intrigued. His predecessor had sneered at da Gama's few ships and cheap goods. Two years later, Cabral appeared with twice as many boats and money.

The zamorin had a proposition for Cabral: A ship smuggling some of his war elephants would soon pass the port, and he wanted Cabral to seize them. Privately, the zamorin did not believe the light Portuguese caravels could do it, but when Cabral succeeded, the zamorin was impressed. Despite his advisers who remembered da Gama, he allowed the Portuguese on land to trade. As soon as they set up their wares, however, angry Muslims instantly overran them. This led to a brawl that killed 50 Portuguese men. In retaliation, Cabral killed or wounded every Muslim on ten to fifteen neighboring ships, and then opened fire on the city—a conflict that took the lives of between 400 and 500 people.

Like da Gama had discovered when he sailed from Mombasa to Malindi, neighboring rulers were often enemies of each other. Cabral headed down the coast to the spice center of Cochin. The city's ruler, a longtime enemy of the ruler of Calicut, met the Portuguese amicably and established a trading agreement. As a result, Cochin became the first official Indian trading post of Portugal. When Cabral returned to Portugal in July 1501, his cargo holds held thousands of pounds of spices.

The Second Voyage

Da Gama's second India-bound fleet left eight months after Cabral's return. This time, da Gama commanded twenty ships, ten for the purposes of trading, and five caravels for attacking rival vessels. The remaining five were military ships that would form the first line of a Portuguese defense fleet off the Indian coast. Like Cabral, da Gama did not hesitate to use force. He set up bases and warehouses at several Muslim ports. He also informed the local rulers that the Portuguese expected not only trade but also yearly tributes (taxes).

On his second voyage to India, in 1502, da Gama had a fleet of twenty ships, most of them Portuguese caravels, like the ones shown in this illustration. The Portuguese were generally regarded as able shipbuilders because they created the smallest and the most maneuverable vessels of the period.

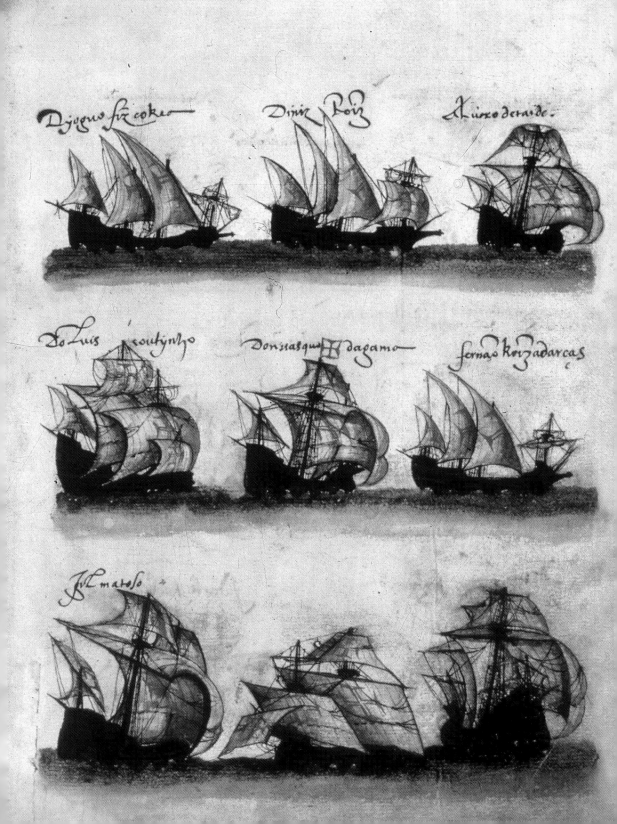

IDOR·DAINDIA·ANODE·502·

Diogvo fr̃ cokeo —   Diniz Roiz   Aluixo deraide·

do Luis coutynho   Don uasques dagamo —   fernão Roizadarcas

Jo̅ marelo·

PEDRO ALVARES CABRAL

Pedro Álvares Cabral, a nobleman with little sailing experience, "discovered" Brazil while on an expedition to India in 1500. He claimed the land for Portugal. Cabral also succeeded where da Gama had not. He established permanent Portuguese trading posts along the Malabar coast in Calicut and Cochin.

In Kilwa, da Gama insisted the sultan raise a flag to show obedience to the Portuguese. On his first voyage, da Gama had felt hounded and deceived. This time he was in control, decisive, and merciless.

In early September 1502, his fleet was off the Malabar coast. Da Gama intended to ambush an Indian spice ship en route from the Red Sea. Because these ships left Arabian seaports with a lot of gold, the take would be enormous. On September 29, the Portuguese spotted the *Mîrî*, a large vessel bound for Calicut. The hundreds of men, women, and children on board had been on a pilgrimage to the Muslim city of Mecca. The Portuguese fired, and though armed, the *Mîrî* did not retaliate.

One of the Indian merchants, Jauhar al-Faqih, made da Gama a generous offer of money and goods, which he refused. Next al-Faqih offered himself as a hostage along with his goods, and the promise to maintain friendly relations. Da Gama remained uninterested. Instead, he retrieved some of the gold from the merchants before ordering his bombardiers to set the *Mîrî* on fire. As the flames caught, the disbelieving Indians fired the few arms they had before throwing rocks at the Portuguese ships. The Portuguese sailed away, but when they saw the Indians had succeeded in putting out the fire, they returned to bombard the ship again. The people cried out for mercy. Women held up their babies. Da Gama's scribe on his second voyage, Tomé Lopes, later said that vengeance was worth more to da Gama than money.

1469 1969

ASIA

Goa

Calicut

Malindi

Mombasa

Mozambique

SOFALA

	First Voyage
First Voyage	Set sail on July 8, 1497 Reached India on May 20, 1498
Second Voyage	Second Voyage Set sail on February 12, 1502 Reached India on October 30, 1502

This map, actually taken from a Portuguese postage stamp commemorating Vasco da Gama's monumental 1497–1498 voyage to India, details his two journeys around the coast of Africa to riches of the east.

Da Gama was determined to prove his power to a country that on his first trip had scorned his lack of wealth and had taken Portuguese lives.

The Indians understood that the conflict was a hopeless one. They threw their wealth into the sea and then rammed and boarded one of the Portuguese ships. They fought ferociously until nightfall, when the rest of the Portuguese fleet managed to pull the ships apart. Impressed by the Indians' courage, Lopes argued with da Gama to spare them, but da Gama wanted to bomb the vessel. The weather, however, made it difficult to get a clean shot. Finally, one of the Indians swam over to the Portuguese and, in exchange for saving his life, told da Gama how to hit the ship. Finally, da Gama fired successfully. In four days, the *Mîrî* and all the people on it burned to the waterline.

When da Gama reached Cannanur on the Malabar coast, the new zamorin of Calicut wrote to him in an attempt to avoid more violence. But da Gama held fast to the memory of Portuguese lives lost at Calicut when Cabral's men were attacked in the marketplace. When the zamorin remarked that the Portuguese losses balanced the damage done by Cabral and to the *Mîrî*, da Gama felt insulted. In a show of anger, he increased his demands. By November 1, he insisted the zamorin exile (forcibly exit) all Middle Eastern Muslims from Calicut. This was an unreasonable— even insane—demand. The zamorin, now

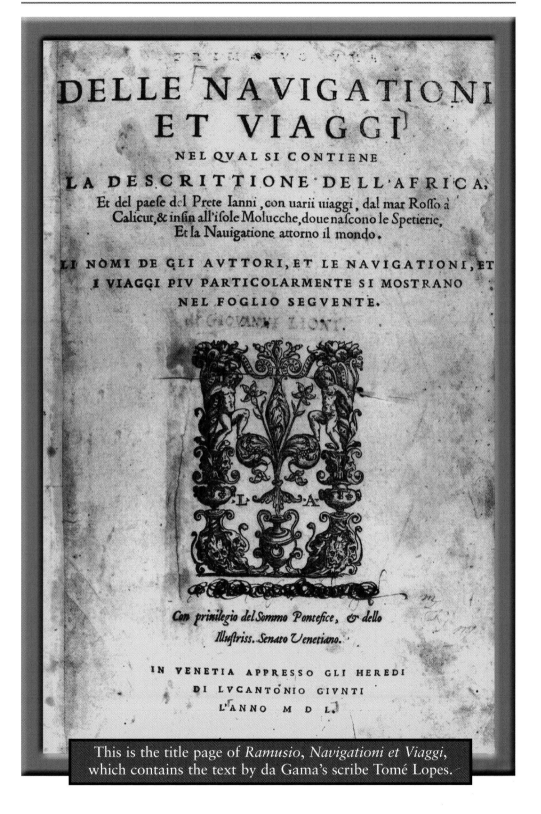

PRIMA VOLTA

DELLE NAVIGATIONI ET VIAGGI.

NEL QVAL SI CONTIENE

LA DESCRITTIONE DELL'AFRICA,

Et del paese del Prete Ianni, con uarii uiaggi, dal mar Rosso à
Calicut, & infin all'ifole Molucche, doue nafcono le Spetierie,
Et la Nauigatione attorno il mondo.

LI NOMI DE GLI AVTTORI, ET LE NAVIGATIONI, ET
I VIAGGI PIV PARTICOLARMENTE SI MOSTRANO
NEL FOGLIO SEGVENTE.

di GIOVANNI LIONI.

L· A·

*Con priuilegio del Sommo Pontefice, & dello
Illuftriss. Senato Venetiano.*

IN VENETIA APPRESSO GLI HEREDI
DI LVCANTONIO GIVNTI
L'ANNO M D L.

This is the title page of *Ramusio, Navigationi et Viaggi,*
which contains the text by da Gama's scribe Tomé Lopes.

The Portuguese ruled Goa, an Indian coastal city whose fruits are depicted here, until 1961—nearly 500 years. During that time, they established trade routes as far east as China and later Japan. By 1557, Portugal had created a permanent colony at Macao, along China's coast, which became the country's point of trading activity in the Far East.

Cajus

Iaquas.

wary of the expertise of Portuguese firepower, for-tified his seafront with a stockade of palm trees. Da Gama waited until midday for a response. When none came, he began to seize passing vessels. Then he ordered his men to hang prisoners from the ships' masts.

By evening, da Gama had hanged thirty-four men. At dusk, he cut off the victims' heads, hands, and feet and sent them by boat to the zamorin with a letter requesting that Calicut surrender. The zamorin refused. As a result, da Gama bombarded the city, destroying all of its houses along the water-front and many of its mansions. Hundreds died. According to Lopes, da Gama fired 400 cannon-balls at the city. Finally, da Gama left six ships and a caravel to maintain a blockade at Calicut's har-bor. His remaining fleet sailed on to Cochin.

At the ports of Cochin, Colon, and Cannanur, da Gama maintained more cordial relations. Cochin, in particular, was the heart of the spice trade and the city in which the Portuguese wanted to establish their business. Here da Gama traded a mix of three-quarters silver and one-quarter copper for pepper. He used fabrics to buy cloves, and brazilwood to buy cinnamon and incense. The fleet set sail for home in the winter of 1503. By early fall, da Gama was back in Lisbon, Portugal's capital city, with a wealth of loot and the news that the country's naval fleet had violently devastated Calicut and its coastline.

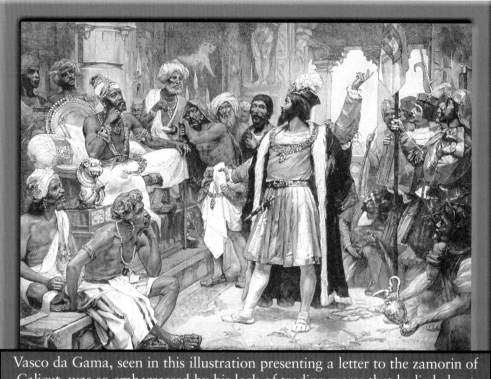

Vasco da Gama, seen in this illustration presenting a letter to the zamorin of Calicut, was so embarrassed by his lack of trading wares that he lied about their origin, telling the leader that the items were actually his own possessions.

Portuguese Sea Violence

Before the Portuguese arrived, trade in the Indian Ocean was stable. Portugal's habitual use of violence destroyed that relative tranquility. For Portuguese captains, any ship that was not an established ally of Portugal's, was fair game for attack. Before the Portuguese attack, piracy in the Indian Ocean had been conducted by outlaws, not supported by a country. Moreover, it occurred away from the land. Ships had only very occasionally attacked cities. There had never before been an organized naval force that attacked so relentlessly and so far from its home base.

ALFONSO de ALBUQUERQUE II. GOVERNOR of INDIA. 1509.

Vasco da Gama did much to advance Portugal's wealth and powers, and he also set a precedent for other Portuguese navigators who followed his lead. Afonso de Albuquerque, pictured in this engraving, was one such person. He seized the port of Goa on the Malabar coast in 1510, making it Portugal's most important trading outpost in India.

Subsequently, the Portuguese devoted the next fifteen years to increasing their grip on the region. For commerce and defense, they established more bases and depots. Offensively, they attacked foreign ports and trade routes. King Manuel appointed Francisco de Almeida the viceroy of the estate of India. De Almeida's attacks on Arabian trading vessels were brutal, often leaving few survivors. To stop rival traders at the source, King Manuel's men fought for control of the passages from the Indian Ocean to the Red Sea.

In 1507, Afonso de Albuquerque (1453–1515) took Hurmuz, the city at the gateway to the Persian Gulf. Turan Shah, the city's ruler, was forced to pay tribute to Portugal. Emboldened by this success, Albuquerque next moved to take the larger city of Aden, which guarded the entrance to the Red Sea. This proved impossible. The Portuguese had disrupted and infiltrated the Muslim trade with Europe but had not entirely destroyed it. Despite this failure at Aden, King Manuel was highly satisfied with his position in the East. When Albuquerque took the city of Goa on the Indian coast in 1510, the king made it his base of operations in what he now described as "Portuguese Asia." From there, it was possible to reach even farther east. The Portuguese at Goa succeeded—at least on a few occasions—to establish trade and missionary relationships with Thailand, China, and eventually Japan.

5

PORTUGUESE ASIA

The Count of Vedigueira in my view understood the affairs of India better than anyone else, and his vote was that Malaca should be sold to the king of Abitão [Bintang], and I do not recall whether with Ormuz [Hormuz] too a similar bargain should be struck, and that these and all the other fortresses in India should be levelled, except Goa and Cochin, it being certain that if in the beginning of the decision to navigate [to India], this had been kept in mind, it would have been wonderful.
—Duke of Bragança, in a letter to King João III, 1529

Portugal had opened a door that could not be closed. It had radically altered its relationships with the countries of Asia, the Middle East, and Europe. By 1505, Portugal began to threaten the Italians, too, jeopardizing Venice's longstanding trading relationships in the East.

Portugal had become a powerful military and economic force, both abroad and at home, but despite its new status, it remained a small country. Portugal had few resources and no major allies. In fact, its main strength was now wealth, and riches alone cannot keep a kingdom safe. Portugal's heady rush of success gave way to a ceaseless struggle to protect its bases and trade routes. At the height of its ambition, Portugal found itself overextended.

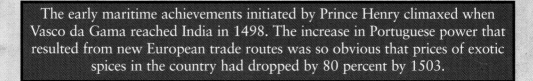

The early maritime achievements initiated by Prince Henry climaxed when Vasco da Gama reached India in 1498. The increase in Portuguese power that resulted from new European trade routes was so obvious that prices of exotic spices in the country had dropped by 80 percent by 1503.

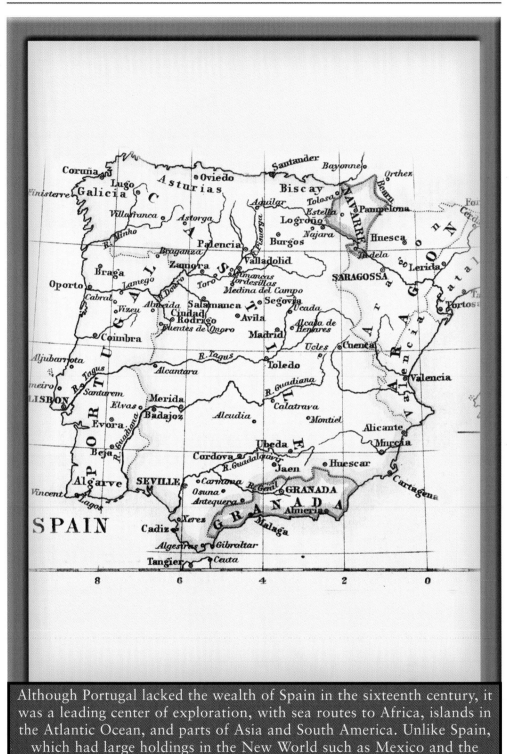

Although Portugal lacked the wealth of Spain in the sixteenth century, it was a leading center of exploration, with sea routes to Africa, islands in the Atlantic Ocean, and parts of Asia and South America. Unlike Spain, which had large holdings in the New World such as Mexico and the western coast of South America to Chile, Portugal did not have the manpower to properly control its new territories.

Once he was back in Lisbon, da Gama withdrew from the political stage. Despite his immense personal wealth, he was dissatisfied. He wanted King Manuel to make him a count, an action the king had mentioned but had never actually granted him.

By 1518, however, the king was struggling to maintain Portugal's power in the East. Seeing an opportunity, da Gama wrote to Manuel stating that if Manuel did not appoint him count of Vidigueira, he would leave Portugal for the service of Charles V (1500–1558), the Hapsburg ruler of Spain.

This was a terrible threat. Spain, alternately an ally and an enemy of Portugal's, was the only other country that laid any claim to the wealth of Asia and the Americas. In 1494, the Treaty of Tordesillas had divided the territories that were still uncharted by Europeans between Portugal and Spain. This arbitrary, now longitudinal (lengthwise) division granted all of the lands to the west, with the exception of the eastern bulge of Brazil, to Spain. The lands to the east belonged to Portugal, which, like Spain, was a Catholic country. In their view, the pope had the power to decide whether one kingdom did or did not have the right to claim the territories and plunder the riches of another.

The Molucca Islands, or Spice Islands, in the East Indies were first encountered by Ferdinand Magellan's crew during his 1511–1512 voyage to circumnavigate the earth. Shortly after, the Portuguese began the process of conquering the valuable island group, beginning a century-long monopoly over the spice trade. This illustration, which depicts village life, was taken from a Dutch book by Jan Huygen van Linschoten. The Dutch took control of the islands from the Portuguese in the seventeenth century and later used their worth when battling with England. To maintain the Dutch monopoly over the spice trade, the Dutch offered the English the island of New Amsterdam, which became New York City in 1664.

t. fecit

For more than a decade, the Portuguese had moved east with complete conviction. Now, the Spanish were questioning the Portuguese claim to the Molucca Islands and petitioning the pope. Da Gama was a major Portuguese hero in this growing rivalry between the two kingdoms. His defection (desertion) to Spain would set a bad example. King Manuel surrendered, and in 1519, da Gama became count of Vidigueira.

Two years later, in December 1521, King Manuel died. His absence revealed the grand scope of Portuguese overextension. In the last year of his reign, he had ordered the construction of a Portuguese fortress in China—something that the Chinese had no intention of allowing. In fact, Portugal barely had the resources to maintain its established eastern position. One critic of this overextension was Aires da Gama, one of Vasco's brothers, who was the captain of Cannanur.

In a 1518 letter to King Manuel, Aires remarked that the Portuguese had too many ships in the Indian Ocean and more officials in Goa than in an area twice the size of Lisbon. His advice was to scale back and center operations at Cochin, which had always been Portugal's most lucrative trading base. Da Gama felt the same. He believed that the consolidation of Portuguese power into no more than two cities—preferably Goa and Cochin— was the best way to maintain a solid grip on the East.

Da Gama's Appointment

During the next two years, Count da Gama emerged as a powerful leader. When the former king's son and successor, João III, appointed him viceroy of the estate of India, da Gama began planning his return. His informants in India described an empire weakened by embezzling

King Charles I of Spain (1516–1556), also Holy Roman Emperor Charles V (1519–1556), was from the house of Hapsburg.

(stealing), bribery, and general corruption. Da Gama intended to weed out the parasites, repair the sagging structure of Portuguese Asia, and defend it from the Spanish and their king, the Hapsburg emperor, Charles V of Austria. Da Gama was personally prepared to kill anyone who attempted to deliver spices to Spain. According to da Gama, the Spanish claim to the Molucca Islands would never be honored.

During this period, many Portuguese nobles saw their kingdom as a sinking ship, making defection to wealthy and powerful Spain even more attractive. But da Gama's loyalty to Portugal never wavered. Either his earlier threats to King Manuel had been purely manipulative, or the reward of his title reinforced his patriotism.

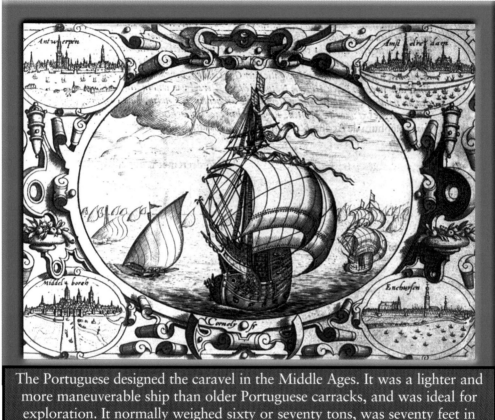

The Portuguese designed the caravel in the Middle Ages. It was a lighter and more maneuverable ship than older Portuguese carracks, and was ideal for exploration. It normally weighed sixty or seventy tons, was seventy feet in length and twenty-five feet abeam, and carried two or three lateen sails.

For the voyage, da Gama's fourteen ships held a crew of 3,000 faithful men, including sailors, soldiers, aristocrats, and his two sons, Estêvão and Paulo. Da Gama planned to strengthen Portuguese power by removing resources from the kingdom's unused fortresses. He would then consolidate the men and supplies in a few well-placed bases, forcing several men to take charge of the ports of Hurmuz, Goa, Cannanur, Cochin, and Molucca. Da Gama also hoped to replace the corrupt governor of Portuguese India, Duarte de Meneses.

6
THE FINAL VOYAGE

Already in this vainglorious business delusions are possessing you,
Already, ferocity and brute force are labelling strength and valour,
The heresy "Long Live Death!" is already current among you,
when life should always be cherished, as Christ in times gone by
Who gave us death yet was afraid to die.
　　　　　　—Excerpt from the epic poem *Os Lusiadas*
　　　　　　(The Lusiads) by Luís Vaz de Camões, 1572

Da Gama's final voyage left Lisbon on April 9, 1524. The fleet stayed off the Portuguese coast for a week. Finally, on April 16, just over twenty-five years after his historic first trip, da Gama headed for the open sea. Portuguese advances were now obvious in the handsome Catholic churches and busy ports that dotted the shoreline.

At first, his voyage seemed ill-fated. One of the galleons hit a reef near Malindi, two were wrecked in the Indian Ocean, and the crew of a fourth mutinied, killing their captain and taking up piracy. In September, an earthquake rocked the seas. Many of the sailors feared this was an evil omen. Then da Gama's luck changed. His fleet looted a Muslim ship filled with gold en route to India. He recorded the loot so as not to be accused of the type of profiteering he was on his way to stop, and then he released the ship.

Da Gama arrived at the Indian port of Chaul and found it in disarray. The Portuguese system was corrupt. Muslims, who objected to the Portuguese presence, worked tirelessly to worsen the corruption. As the new viceroy, da Gama took a swift account of the salaries in the Portuguese fortress. He dismissed anyone he viewed as a financial parasite. Next, he sailed to the port city of Goa, where he made similar changes, replacing officials and auditing expenses. Da Gama impressed the Goans with his fairness. Unlike previous officials, he refused to take gifts, showing that he would be difficult to bribe.

Although fair and incorruptible in some ways, da Gama was merciless to the disobedient. In Goa, he discovered two Portuguese women who had hidden themselves in a ship so they could meet their fiancés in India. He had them whipped publicly. When they protested that no one would marry them after such humiliation, he ignored their pleas. (According to the historian Gaspar Correia, da Gama sent the women monetary compensation from his deathbed.) Da Gama was also unsympathetic to men who lacked visible injuries. He classed them as shirkers (people who avoid obligations) and terminated the pensions of soldiers who were unable to fight.

Da Gama continued down the coast to Cochin but faced endless problems as a viceroy. The Mappila merchants on the Malabar coast who sold pepper to

This portrait of Vasco da Gama was made around 1524, before his last voyage to India, and shortly before his unexpected death that same year on December 24, Christmas Eve.

Portugal often mixed it with sand. By the time the pepper was cleaned, the Portuguese sustained losses of 30 or 40 percent. Another problem was Calicut. Relations had not improved since Cabral's attacks. King João wanted da Gama to bring the city under Portuguese control. But da Gama, at that time in his mid-fifties, was aging. The tropical climate had weakened him. Soon he moved to a quiet house on the outskirts of Cochin and ceded more responsibility to the captain of Cochin, Lopo Vaz de Sampaio.

Da Gama died just three months after his arrival, on Christmas Eve 1524. Honored with a grand ceremony, he was laid to rest at the Franciscan church of Santo António, one of the first Portuguese churches in Asia. Ten years later, his body was returned to Portugal and buried in Vidigueira, the lands of which King Manuel had made him count. More than 350 years later, his body was moved yet again, this time to the Jeronimos Monastery near Lisbon. It now lies near King Manuel and the original launching place of the *São Gabriel*.

The Myth

The 500th anniversary of da Gama's arrival in Calicut was on May 22, 1998. Portugal spared no expense in honoring its national hero, whose glorification had begun five centuries ago. Praising da Gama as a peerless symbol of Portuguese intelligence and tenacity, the country celebrated his impact on world culture.

Originally buried in India, Vasco da Gama's remains were moved twice and are now housed in Lisbon. His ornate marble tomb *(above)* is located in the Monastery of Jeronimos.

In other countries, scholars discussed da Gama in less glowing terms. Mozambicans were unenthusiastic about commemorating a man associated with the subject of the slave trade. In India, opponents of the celebrations denounced da Gama as a pirate, decrying his bombardment of Calicut (now called Kozhikode, in the southern state of Kerala) and his sale of thousands of Indians into slavery. Others defended him. He was no more violent than other explorers and conquistadors—Hernán Cortés, Francisco Pizarro—that Renaissance Europe unleashed on the rest of the world. Moreover, da Gama's sea passage ushered in a new age of cultural exchange.

Calcoen

A DUTCH NARRATIVE OF THE SECOND VOYAGE

OF VASCO DA GAMA TO

CALICUT

Printed at Antwerp circa 1504

WITH INTRODUCTION AND TRANSLATION

BY J. Ph. BERJEAU

ALDI

DISCIP.

ANGLVS

LONDON

BASIL MONTAGU PICKERING

196 PICCADILLY

1874

This is the title page of a book chronicling da Gama's second voyage to India.

Adversaries also pointed out that da Gama's route was not a discovery. What the Portuguese "discovered" along the African coastline or in the Indian Ocean had been known to Arabian and Chinese navigators for centuries. The Indian Ocean crossing, in fact, was well traveled by such Asians as the Gujarati pilot da Gama hired in Malindi. Da Gama had only linked the routes revealed by other explorers.

It is easy to see what went wrong following da Gama's arrival on the Indian coast. What would have happened, had he failed, is open to speculation. It is likely that another Portuguese explorer, such as Ferdinand Magellan, would have taken his place. Certainly, da Gama was not personally responsible for the ceaseless march of conquistadors and missionaries around the globe.

Unlike Bartolomeu Dias, da Gama had the strength of will to lead his men to the end point of a brutal journey. He also had the immorality to burn the *Mîrî*. The decision to celebrate or denounce him is complex. His worthy actions cannot be separated from his despicable ones.

The tale of da Gama's voyage is a tapestry of recorded facts, hearsay, and emotional impressions. If his strengths illustrate human achievement, then perhaps his crimes can be a warning for the future.

CHRONOLOGY

1385   King João I, father of the Noble Generation, takes the Portuguese throne.

1394   King João's wife, Queen Philippa, gives birth to Prince Henry the Navigator.

1415   Princes Henry, Edward, and Pedro conquer the city of Ceuta in North Africa.

1419   Henry makes his first exploratory voyage down the West African coast.

1433   Under the command of Gil Eanes, one of Henry's ships passes Cape Bojador.

1445   More than two dozen Portuguese slave traders embark for West Africa.

1446   West African archers kill four and wound fourteen of Nuno Tristão's men on the Gambia River.

1460   Prince Henry dies at Sages.

1460   Approximate date of Vasco da Gama's birth.

1481   King João II takes the throne, and during his reign establishes posts in regions of Africa now known as Ghana, Angola, and Zaire.

1488   Bartolomeu Dias rounds the Cape of Good Hope.

1492   Vasco da Gama mounts a successful attack against several French ships.

1494   The Treaty of Tordesillas divides the world between Portugal and Spain.

1495   King João II dies, and the throne passes to King Manuel.

1497   Vasco da Gama sets sail for the East.

1498   Vasco da Gama reaches India.

1499   Vasco da Gama returns to Lisbon, Portugal.

1500   Pedro Cabral lands in Brazil and claims it for Portugal.

1501   Pedro Cabral reaches India.

1502   Vasco da Gama begins his second voyage to India.

1505   Portugal begins to threaten Venetian interests in the East.

1507   Afonso de Albuquerque takes Hurmuz, the gateway city to the Persian Gulf.

1508   Afonso de Albuquerque fails to take Aden, gateway to the Red Sea.

1518   Aires da Gama writes to King Manuel that Portuguese Asia is overextended.

1519   Vasco da Gama becomes the count of Vidigueira.

1521   King Manuel dies, and the throne passes to King João III.

1524   Vasco da Gama's last voyage to India ends with his death in Cochin on December 24.

GLOSSARY

betel The seed of a pepper plant, chewed in South Asia.

bombardier An artillery soldier who fires guns or cannons.

brazilwood A very heavy, reddish wood used for cabinet work and dyeing; King Manuel named the country of Brazil for its production of this wood.

caravel A small, light sailing ship with two or three masts and lateen sails.

carrack A large galleon of the fourteenth, fifteenth, and sixteenth centuries.

circumnavigate To proceed completely around; to circle, as in a continent or Earth.

corsair A pirate, originally on North Africa's Barbary Coast, now in general usage.

degredado A convict-exile taken on sea voyages to perform dangerous tasks.

duties Taxes charged by a government on imports.

fleet A group of ships operating under one command.

galleon A large, three-masted sailing ship with a square rig and two or more decks.

ghat A broad flight of steps. The term refers to the two mountain ranges of South India, paralleling the western coast of the Arabian Sea and eastern coast of the Bay of Bengal. It can also mean the steps along a riverbank used by bathers.

infidel An unbeliever with respect to a particular religion, usually Christianity or Islam.

Islam A monotheistic religion in which Muhammad is the chief and last prophet of God.

lateen A triangular sail on a long beam attached at an angle to the top of a short mast.

latitude The distance on Earth's surface north or south from the equator.

longitude The distance on Earth's surface east or west from Greenwich, England.

missionary One who attempts to convert others to a particular religion.

rutter A sailing manual containing charts and records of routes to certain destinations.

scribe A person who makes written copies of documents and manuscripts.

scurvy A disease caused by lack of vitamin C and marked by swollen gums and livid spots.

stockade A defensive barrier of posts driven upright side by side into the ground.

sultan A ruler of a Muslim country.

treaty A formal agreement describing terms of peace, trade, or territorial right.

FOR MORE
INFORMATION

The Mariners' Museum
100 Museum Drive
Newport News, VA 23606
(757) 596-2222
Web site: http://www.mariner.org

The National Maritime Museum
Greenwich, London
SE10 9NF
England
(+44) 020 8858 4422
Web site: http://www.nmm.ac.uk

Web Sites

Due to the changing nature of Internet links, the Rosen
Publishing Group, Inc., has developed an online list
of Web sites related to the subject of this book. This
site is updated regularly. Please use this link to
access the list:

http://www.rosenlinks.com/lee/vaga/

FOR FURTHER READING

Bohlander, Richard E. *World Explorers and Discoverers.* New York: Da Capo Press, 1998.

Gallagher, Jim. *Vasco da Gama and the Portuguese Explorers* (Explorers of the New World). Broomall, PA: Chelsea House, 2000.

Goodman, Joan Elizabeth. *A Long and Uncertain Journey: The 27,000 Mile Voyage of Vasco da Gama* (Great Explorers). New York: Mikaya Press, 2001.

Hemming, John, ed. *Atlas of Exploration.* New York: Oxford University Press, 1997.

Mattern, Joanne, and Patrick O'Brien (illustrator). *The Travels of Vasco da Gama.* Chatham, NJ: Raintree/Steck-Vaughn, 2000.

Stefoff, Rebecca. *Accidental Explorers: Surprises and Side Trips in the History of Discovery.* New York: Oxford University Press, 1992.

Stefoff, Rebecca, and William H. Goetzmann, eds. *Vasco da Gama and the Portuguese Explorers.* Broomall, PA: Chelsea House, 1993.

BIBLIOGRAPHY

Baker, Daniel B., ed. *Explorers and Discoverers of the World*. Detroit, MI: Gale Research, 1993.

Barraclough, Geoffrey, ed. *The Times Atlas of World History*. New York: Hammond, 1984.

Bell, Christopher. *Portugal and the Quest for the Indies*. New York: Barnes & Noble, 1974.

Boorstin, Daniel J. *The Discoverers: A History of Man's Search to Know His World and Himself*. New York: Vintage Books, 1985.

Camões, Luís Vaz de. *Os Lusiades* (The Lusiads). English translation by William C. Atkinson. London: Penguin Books, 1952.

Cuyvers, Luc. *Into the Rising Sun: Vasco da Gama and the Search for the Sea Route to the East*. New York: TV Books, 1999.

Goodman, Joan Elizabeth. *A Long and Uncertain Journey: The 27,000 Mile Voyage of Vasco da Gama*. (Great Explorers). New York: Mikaya Press, 2001.

Hemming, John, ed. *Atlas of Exploration*. New York: Oxford University Press, 1997.

Madan, D. K. *Life and Letters of Vasco da Gama*. Columbia, MO: South Asia Books, 1998.

Mattern, Joanne, and Patrick O'Brien (illustrator). *The Travels of Vasco da Gama*. Chatham, NJ: Raintree/Steck-Vaughn, 2000.

Pearson, M. N. *The Portuguese in India*. Cambridge, England: Cambridge University Press, 1987.

Stefoff, Rebecca, and William H. Goetzmann, eds. *Vasco da Gama and the Portuguese Explorers*. Broomall, PA: Chelsea House, 1993.

Subrahmanyam, Sanjay. *The Career and Legend of Vasco da Gama*. New York: Cambridge University Press, 1997.

Velho, Álvaro (attributed). *A Journal of the First Voyage of Vasco da Gama, 1497–1499*. London: Hakluyt Society Publications, 1st ser., vol. 99., 1898.

INDEX

Index

About the Author

Allison Stark Draper has written books about history and science for young readers. She lives in Stone Ridge, New York.

Photo Credits

Cover © Greenwich Hospital Collection/National Maritime Museum; pp. 4, 56–57, 68, 74–75 © The Granger Collection; pp. 9, 27, 36 © The Mariners' Museum, Newport News, VA; pp. 11, 14, 16 © Hulton/Archive/Getty Images; pp. 18–19 © Alinari/Art Resource; pp. 22, 51, 94 © Giraudon/Art Resource; p. 24 © Mary Evans Picture Library; pp. 28–29 Courtesy Bibliotheque National de France; p. 33 © Scala/Art Resource; p. 39 © Library of Congress, Prints & Photographs Division; p. 43 © British Library; p. 46 © Super Stock; p. 53 © North Wind Picture Archives; p. 59 © Art Resource; p. 62 © Mansell/Timepix; pp. 65, 77 Courtesy James Ford Bell Library, University of Minnesota; pp. 70–71, 85 © The Pierpont Morgan Library/Art Resource; p. 72 © Corbis; pp. 78–79, 88–89, 92, 98 Rare Books and Manuscript Division, The New York Public Library, Astor, Lenox and Tilden Foundations; pp. 81, 82, 91 © Bettmann/Corbis; p. 86 © North Wind Picture Archives; p. 97 © Bernard Hoffman/Timepix.

Series Design and Layout

Tahara Hasan

Editor

Joann Jovinelly